Air fryer toaster oven cookbook

Effortless, Quick and Easy Air Fryer Toaster Oven Recipes for Everyone

Nichole S. Rodriguez

TABLE OF CONTENTS

INTRODUCTION

The secret of Air Fryer is the unique cooking technology that uses hot-air that circulates inside the fryer. It works no different than any other thermic-processing method, but without all the detrimental side-effects you get when you eat deep-fried foods, for example. You may be able not only to fry but also to bake, broil, roast, rotisserie, and steam things as well. Air Fryer can also be a great substitute for your microwave, oven, or a stove. Except it's much healthier, easier, and faster to use.

Needless to say, as you reduce the amount of fat in your meals, their calorific value drops as well. So not only you eat overall healthier but even your "cheat meals" are less of a problem now. As you can see, using an air fryer can effectively help you drop some extra weight. Maybe it's time you reinstated your relationship with French fries?

It's compact, and it fits everywhere

Because it takes so little space on the kitchen countertop, you don't have to worry about additional clutter. It also doesn't kill the aesthetics of your countertop. You can also put all the accessories inside the fryer, so you reduce unnecessary mess to a 0 level. See how you can start enjoying being in the kitchen again.

How to use an air fryer?

Prepare the air fryer

Some recipes will require using a basket, a rack, or a rotisserie. Some other recipes require cake or muffin pans. Before you pick the recipe and prepare your accessories, make sure they fit into your fryer.

Prepare the ingredients

Once you have all that's necessary to prepare your recipe, place the ingredients directly inside the appliance or use a basket, a rack, or a pan to do so. To prevent sticking use parchment baking paper or simply spray the food with a little bit of oil. A word of caution is necessary here. Never over-stuff the chamber with too much food. It will not cook to an equal measure, and you may find yourself getting frustrated chewing under-cooked bits. If you're planning on cooking more, multiple rounds of air-frying may be necessary.

Set the temperature and time

Most of Air Fryers use pre-set modes depending on the type of recipe. You can adjust settings such as time and temperature manually to make the best use of your recipes.

Check food during cooking

Many recipes will require you to control from time to time the content of your fryer while cooking. This is to make sure everything gets cooked evenly. Normally all it takes is to shake or flip the food to distribute it. For some recipes, however, you'll need to turn the food around some time halfway through the cooking.

Cleaning time

Before you start cleaning, plug the air fryer off and let it cool down. Once it's ready, stick to instructions you got from the manufacturer and never scrub or use any other abrasive material on the inner surface of the chamber.

BREAKFAST RECIPES

1. Cheddar Soufflé with Herbs

Preparation time: 10 minutes

Cooking time: 8 minutes

Servings: 4

Ingredients:

- 5 oz. Cheddar cheese, shredded

- 3 eggs

- 4 tablespoons heavy cream

- 1 tablespoon chives

- 1 tablespoon dill

- 1 teaspoon parsley

- ½ teaspoon ground thyme

Directions:

1. Crack the eggs into a bowl and whisk them carefully.

2. Add the heavy cream and whisk it for 10 seconds more.

3. Add the chives, dill, parsley, and ground thyme.

4. Sprinkle the egg mixture with the shredded cheese and stir it.

5. Transfer the egg mixture into 4 ramekins and place the ramekins in the air fryer basket.

6. Preheat the air fryer to 390 F and cook the soufflé for 8 minutes.

7. Once cooked, chill well.

Nutrition: calories 244 fat 20.6 fiber 0.2 carbs 1.7 protein 13.5

2. <u>Bacon Butter Biscuits</u>

Preparation time: 15 minutes

Cooking time: 10 minutes

Servings: 6

Ingredients:

- 1 egg

- 4 oz. bacon, cooked

- 1 cup almond flour

- ½ teaspoon baking soda

- 1 tablespoon apple cider vinegar

- 3 tablespoon butter

- 4 tablespoons heavy cream

- 1 teaspoon dried oregano

Directions:

1. Crack the egg in a bowl and whisk it.

2. Chop the cooked bacon and add it into the whisked egg.

3. Sprinkle the mixture with baking soda and apple cider vinegar.

4. Add the heavy cream and dried oregano. Stir.

5. Add butter and almond flour.

6. Mix well with a hand mixer.

7. When you get a smooth and liquid batter – the dough is cooked.

8. Preheat the air fryer to 400 F.

9. Pour the batter dough into muffin molds.

10. When the air fryer is heated put the muffin molds in the air fryer basket and cook them for 10 minutes.

11. Chill the muffins to room temperature.

Nutrition: calories 226 fat 20.5 fiber 0.6 carbs 1.8 protein 9.2

3. <u>Keto Parmesan Frittata</u>

Preparation time: 10 minutes

Cooking time: 15 minutes

Servings: 6

Ingredients:

- 6 eggs

- 1/3 cup heavy cream

- 1 tomato

- 5 oz. chive stems

- 1 tablespoon butter

- 1 teaspoon salt

- 1 tablespoon dried oregano

- 6 oz. Parmesan

- 1 teaspoon chili pepper

Directions:

1. Crack the eggs into the air fryer basket tray and whisk them with a hand whisker.

2. Chop the tomato and dice the chives.

3. Add the vegetables to the egg mixture.

4. Pour the heavy cream.

5. Sprinkle the liquid mixture with the butter, salt, dried oregano, and chili pepper.

6. Shred Parmesan cheese and add it to the mixture too.

7. Sprinkle the mixture with a silicone spatula.

8. Preheat the air fryer to 375 F and cook the frittata for 15 minutes.

Nutrition: calories 202, fat 15, fiber 0.7, carbs 3.4, protein 15.1

4. Chicken Liver Pate

Preparation time: 10 minutes

Cooking time: 10 minutes

Servings: 7

Ingredients:

- 1-pound chicken liver
- 1 teaspoon salt
- 4 tablespoon butter
- 1 cup water
- 1 teaspoon ground black pepper
- 5 oz. chive stems
- ½ teaspoon dried cilantro

Directions:

1. Chop the chicken liver roughly and place it in the air fryer basket tray.

2. Dice the chives.

3. Pour the water in the air fryer basket tray and add the diced chives.

4. Preheat the air fryer to 360 F and cook the chicken liver for 10 minutes.

5. Once cooked, strain the chicken liver mixture to discard the liquid.

6. Transfer the chicken liver into a blender.

7. Add the butter, ground black pepper, and dried cilantro.

8. Blend the mixture till you get the pate texture.

9. Transfer the liver pate to a bowl and serve it immediately or keep in the fridge.

Nutrition: calories 173fat 10.8 fiber 0.4 carbs 2.2 protein 16.1

5. Coconut Pancake Hash

Preparation time: 7 minutes

Cooking time: 9 minutes

Servings: 9

Ingredients:

- 1 teaspoon baking soda

- 1 tablespoon apple cider vinegar

- 1 teaspoon salt

- 1 teaspoon ground ginger

- 1 cup coconut flour

- 5 tablespoon butter

- 1 egg

- ¼ cup heavy cream

Directions:

1. Combine the baking soda, salt, ground ginger, and flour in a bowl.

2. Take a separate bowl and crack in the egg.

3. Add butter and heavy cream.

4. Use a hand mixer and mix well.

5. Combine the dry and liquid mixture together and stir it until smooth.

6. Preheat the air fryer to 400 F.

7. Pour the pancake mixture into the air fryer basket tray.

8. Cook the pancake hash for 4 minutes.

9. Scramble the pancake hash well and keep cooking for 5 minutes more.

10. Transfer to serving plates and serve hot.

Nutrition: calories 148 fat 11.3 fiber 5.3 carbs 8.7 protein 3.7

MAIN DISH

6. Bacon Wings

Preparation time: 15 minutes

Cooking time: 1 hour 15 minutes

Servings: 12

Ingredients:

- Bacon strips (12 pieces)

- Paprika (1 teaspoon)

- Black pepper (1 tablespoon)

- Oregano (1 teaspoon)

- Chicken wings (12 pieces)

- Kosher salt (1 tablespoon)

- Brown sugar (1 tablespoon)

- Chili powder (1 teaspoon)

- Celery sticks

- Blue cheese dressing

Directions:

1. Preheat the air fryer at 325 degrees Fahrenheit.

2. Mix sugar, salt, chili powder, oregano, pepper, and paprika. Coat chicken wings with this dry rub.

3. Wrap a bacon strip around each wing. Arrange wrapped wings in the air fryer basket.

4. Cook for thirty minutes on each side in the air fryer. Let cool for five minutes.

5. Serve and enjoy with celery and blue cheese.

Nutrition: Calories 100 Fat 5.0 g Protein 10.0 g Carbohydrates 2.0 g

7. Pepper Pesto Lamb

Preparation time: 15 minutes

Cooking time: 1 hour 15 minutes

Servings: 12

Ingredients:

- Pesto

- Rosemary leaves, fresh (1/4 cup)

- Garlic cloves (3 pieces)

- Parsley, fresh, packed firmly (3/4 cup)

- Minutest leaves, fresh (1/4 cup)

- Olive oil (2 tablespoons)

- Lamb

- Red bell peppers, roasted, drained (7 ½ ounces)

- Leg of lamb, boneless, rolled (5 pounds)

- Seasoning, lemon pepper (2 teaspoons)

Directions:

1. Preheat the oven at 325 degrees Fahrenheit.

2. Mix the pesto ingredients in the food processor.

3. Unroll the lamb and cover the cut side with pesto. Top with roasted peppers before rolling up the lamb and tying with kitchen twine.

4. Coat lamb with seasoning (lemon pepper) and air-fry for one hour.

Nutrition: Calories 310 Fat 15.0 g Protein 40.0 g Carbohydrates 1.0 g

8. Tuna Spinach Casserole

Preparation time: 30 minutes

Cooking time: 25 minutes

Servings: 8

Ingredients:

- Mushroom soup, creamy (18 ounces)

- Milk (1/2 cup)

- White tuna, solid, in-water, drained (12 ounces)

- Crescent dinner rolls, refrigerated (8 ounces)

- Egg noodles, wide, uncooked (8 ounces)

- Cheddar cheese, shredded (8 ounces)

- Spinach, chopped, frozen, thawed, drained (9 ounces)

- Lemon peel grated (2 teaspoons)

Directions:

1. Preheat the oven at 350 degrees Fahrenheit.

2. Mist cooking spray onto a glass baking dish (11x7-inch).

3. Follow package directions in cooking and draining the noodles.

4. Stir the cheese (1 ½ cups) and soup together in a skillet heated on medium. Once cheese melts, stir in your noodles, milk, spinach, tuna, and lemon peel. Once bubbling, pour into the prepped dish.

5. Unroll the dough and sprinkle with remaining cheese (1/2 cup). Roll up dough and pinch at the seams to seal. Slice into 8 portions and place over the tuna mixture.

6. Air-fry for twenty to twenty-five minutes.

Nutrition: Calories 400 Fat 19.0 g Protein 21.0 g Carbohydrates 35.0 g

9. Greek Style Mini Burger Pies

Preparation time: 15 minutes

Cooking time: 40 minutes

Servings: 6

Ingredients:

- Burger mixture:

- Onion, large, chopped (1 piece)

- Red bell peppers, roasted, diced (1/2 cup)

- Ground lamb, 80% lean (1 pound)

- Red pepper flakes (1/4 teaspoon)

- Feta cheese, crumbled (2 ounces)

- Baking mixture

- Milk (1/2 cup)

- Biscuit mix, classic (1/2 cup)

- Eggs (2 pieces)

Directions:

1. Preheat the air fryer at 350 degrees Fahrenheit.

2. Grease 12 muffin cups using cooking spray.

3. Cook the onion and beef in a skillet heated on medium-high. Once beef is browned and cooked through, drain and let cool for five minutes.

4. Stir together with feta cheese, roasted red peppers, and red pepper flakes.

5. Whisk the baking mixture ingredients together. Fill each muffin cup with baking mixture (1 tablespoon).

6. Air-fry for twenty-five to thirty minutes. Let cool before serving.

Nutrition: Calories 270 Fat 15.0 g Protein 19.0 g Carbohydrates 13.0 g

10. Family Fun Pizza

Preparation time: 30 min

Cooking time: 25 min

Servings: 16

Ingredients:

- Pizza crust

- Water, warm (1 cup)

- Salt (1/2 teaspoon)

- Flour, whole wheat (1 cup)

- Olive oil (2 tablespoons)

- Dry yeast, quick active (1 package)

- Flour, all purpose (1 ½ cups)

- Cornmeal

- Olive oil

- Filling:

- Onion, chopped (1 cup)

- Mushrooms, sliced, drained (4 ounces)

- Garlic cloves, chopped finely (2 pieces)

- Parmesan cheese, grated (1/4 cup)

- Ground lamb, 80% lean (1 pound)

- Italian seasoning (1 teaspoon)

- Pizza sauce (8 ounces)

- Mozzarella cheese, shredded (2 cups)

Directions:

1. Mix yeast with warm water. Combine with flours, oil (2 tablespoons), and salt by stirring and then beating vigorously for half a minute. Let the dough sit for twenty minutes.

2. Preheat the air fryer at 350 degrees Fahrenheit.

3. Prep 2 square pans (8-inch) by greasing with oil before sprinkling with cornmeal. Cut the rested dough in half; place each half inside each pan. Set aside, covered, for thirty to forty-five minutes. Cook in the air fryer for twenty to twenty-two minutes. Sauté the onion, beef, garlic, and Italian seasoning until beef is completely cooked. Drain and set aside. Cover the air-fried crusts with pizza sauce before topping with beef mixture, cheeses, and mushrooms.

4. Return to the air fryer and cook for twenty minutes.

Nutrition: Calories 215 Fat 10.0 g Protein 13.0 g Carbohydrates 20.0 g

11. Crispy Hot Sauce Chicken

Preparation Time: 5 minutes

Cooking Time: 30 minutes

Servings: 4

Ingredients:

- 2 cups buttermilk

- 1 tablespoon. hot sauce

- 1 whole chicken, cut up

- 1 cup Kentucky Kernel flour

- Oil for spraying

Directions:

1. Whisk hot sauce with buttermilk in a large bowl.

2. Add chicken pieces to the buttermilk mixture and marinate for 1 hour in the refrigerator.

3. Dredge the chicken through seasoned flour and shake off the excess.

4. Place the coated chicken in the air fryer basket and spray them with cooking oil.

5. Return the fryer basket to the air fryer and cook on air fry mode for 30 minutes at 380 degrees F.

6. Flip the chicken pieces once cooked half way through.

7. Enjoy right away.

Nutrition: Calories 695 Total Fat 17.5 g Saturated Fat 4.8 g

SIDE DISHES

12. Cheddar Portobello Mushrooms

Preparation time: 15 minutes

Cooking time: 6 minutes

Servings: 2

Ingredients:

- 2 Portobello mushroom hats

- 2 slices Cheddar cheese

- ¼ cup panko breadcrumbs

- ½ teaspoon salt

- ½ teaspoon ground black pepper

- 1 egg

- 1 teaspoon oatmeal

- 2 oz. bacon, chopped cooked

Directions:

1. Crack the egg into the bowl and whisk it.

2. Combine the ground black pepper, oatmeal, salt, and breadcrumbs in the separate bowl.

3. Dip the mushroom hats in the whisked egg.

4. After this, coat the mushroom hats in the breadcrumb mixture.

5. Preheat the air fryer to 400 F.

6. Place the mushrooms in the air fryer basket tray and cook for 3 minutes.

7. After this, put the chopped bacon and sliced cheese over the mushroom hats and cook the meal for 3 minutes.

8. When the meal is cooked – let it chill gently.

9. Enjoy!

Nutrition: calories 376, fat 24.1, fiber 1.8, carbs 14.6, protein 25.2

13. Air Fried French Fries

Preparation Time: 5 minutes

Cooking Time: 29 minutes

Servings: 3

Ingredients:

- Potatoes – 3

- Olive oil – 3 teaspoons

- Salt - ½ teaspoon

Directions:

1. Peel and wash the potatoes.

2. Cut the potatoes into half inch sticks.

3. Boil a bowl of salted water

4. Blanch the potato cuts for four minutes in the boiling salt water.

5. Drain the potato cuts and pat dry.

6. Set the air fryer temperature to 200 degrees Celsius and preheat for 2 minutes.

7. Pour olive oil into the potato cuts and toss.

8. Place the oil coated potatoes in the air fryer basket.

9. Air fry it for 25 minutes.

10. Shake the air fryer basket intermittently after every 5 minutes.

11. Drizzle salt in the middle of the frying for seasoning.

12. Serve it along with ketchup, shredded parmesan cheese, or mayonnaise, and lemon zest.

Nutrition: Calories 187 Carbohydrates: 33.5g Cholesterol: 0mg Dietary Fiber: 5.1g Fat: 4.9g Sodium: 400mg

14. Air Fried Brussels Sprouts

Preparation Time: 5 minutes

Cooking Time: 10 minutes

Servings: 2

Ingredients:

- Brussels sprouts, cut into halves – 2 cups

- Balsamic vinegar – 1 tablespoon

- Olive oil – 1 tablespoon

- Salt - ¼ teaspoon

Directions:

1. In a medium bowl, add vinegar, olive oil, salt and combine.Add the halved Brussels sprouts into the bowl mix and toss to coat evenly.Place the coated Brussels sprouts in the air fryer basket.Set the temperature at 200 degrees Celsius for 10 minutes.Shake the air fryer basket every 3-4 minutes so that you can have an even cooking.

2. Once done, serve hot.

Nutrition: Calories: 100 Carbohydrate: 8.1g Cholesterol: 0mg Fat: 7.3g Sodium: 73mg Dietary Fiber: 3.3g

15. Air Fried Breaded Mushrooms

Preparation Time: 10 minutes

Cooking Time: 7 minutes

Servings: 4-6

Ingredients:

- Button mushrooms - ½ pound

- Egg – 1 large

- Grated cheese – 3 ounces

- Breadcrumbs – as required to coat

- Flour – as necessary to coat

- Ground pepper - ¼ teaspoon

- Salt – 1/8 teaspoon

Directions:

1. In a medium bowl combine bread crumbs with grated cheese and keep it aside.

2. Now beat the egg in another medium bowl and keep it aside.

3. Wash the mushrooms and dry pat.

4. Put the flour in a flat plate and roll the mushroom in the flour.

5. Dip the flour rolled mushroom in the beaten egg.

6. Now dip the mushroom again in the cheese & bread crumb mixture.

7. Place the coated mushroom in the air fryer cooking basket.

8. Set the temperature at 180 degrees Celsius and timer for 7 minutes.

9. Shake the air fryer basket in between 3-4 times so that it can have an even frying.

10. Serve hot along with any dipping sauce.

Nutrition: Calories: 169 Carbohydrate: 13g Cholesterol: 63mg Fat: 8.7g Sodium: 204mg Dietary Fiber: 1.1g

SEAFOOD RECIPES

16. Pesto Salmon

Preparation Time: 10 minutes

Cooking Time: 16 minutes

Servings: 4

Ingredients:

- 25 oz. salmon fillet

- 1 tablespoon. green pesto

- 1 cup mayonnaise

- 1/2 oz. olive oil

- 1 lb. fresh spinach

- 2 oz. parmesan cheese, grated

- Pepper

- Salt

Directions:

1. Preheat the air fryer to 370 F.

2. Spray air fryer basket with cooking spray.

3. Season salmon fillet with pepper and salt and place into the air fryer basket.

4. In a bowl, mix together mayonnaise, parmesan cheese, and pesto and spread over the salmon fillet.

5. Cook salmon for 14-16 minutes.

6. Meanwhile, in a pan sauté spinach with olive oil until spinach is wilted, about 2-3 minutes. Season with pepper and salt.

7. Transfer spinach in serving plate and top with cooked salmon.

8. Serve and enjoy.

Nutrition: Calories 545 Fat 39.6 g Carbohydrates 9.5 g Sugar 3.1 g Protein 43 g Cholesterol 110 mg

17. Parmesan Walnut Salmon

Preparation Time: 10 minutes

Cooking Time: 12 minutes

Servings: 4

Ingredients:

- 4 salmon fillets

- 1/4 cup parmesan cheese, grated

- 1/2 cup walnuts

- 1 teaspoon olive oil

- 1 tablespoon. lemon rind

Directions:

1. Preheat the air fryer to 370 F.

2. Spray an air fryer baking dish with cooking spray.

3. Place salmon on a baking dish.

4. Add walnuts into the food processor and process until finely ground.

5. Mix ground walnuts with parmesan cheese, oil, and lemon rind. Stir well.

6. Spoon walnut mixture over the salmon and press gently.

7. Place in the air fryer and cook for 12 minutes.

8. Serve and enjoy.

Nutrition: Calories 420 Fat 27.4 g Carbohydrates 2 g Sugar 0.3 g

Protein 46.3 g Cholesterol 98 mg

18. Lemon Shrimp

Preparation Time: 10 minutes

Cooking Time: 8 minutes

Servings: 2

Ingredients:

- 12 oz. shrimp, peeled and deveined

- 1 lemon sliced

- 1/4 teaspoon garlic powder

- 1/4 teaspoon paprika

- 1 teaspoon lemon pepper

- 1 lemon juice

- 1 tablespoon. olive oil

Directions:

1. In a bowl, mix together oil, lemon juice, garlic powder, paprika, and lemon pepper.

2. Add shrimp to the bowl and toss well to coat.

3. Spray air fryer basket with cooking spray.

4. Transfer shrimp into the air fryer basket and cook at 400 F for 8 minutes.

5. Garnish with lemon slices and serve.

Nutrition: Calories 381 Fat 17.1 g Carbohydrates 4.1 g Sugar 0.6 g Protein 50.6 g Cholesterol 358 mg

19. Fish & Chips

Preparation time: 10 minutes

Cooking time: 20 minutes

Servings: 4

Ingredients:

- 2 tablespoon. olive oil

- 4 potatoes, cut into thin slices

- Salt and black pepper to taste

- 4 white fish fillets

- 1 cup flour

- 2 eggs, beaten

- 1 cup breadcrumbs

- Salt and black pepper

Directions:

1. Drizzle potatoes with olive oil and season with salt and black pepper; toss to coat. Place them in the air fryer and Air Fry for 10 minutes at 400 F.

2. Season the fillets with salt and pepper. Coat them with flour, then dip in the eggs, and finally into the crumbs.

3. Shake the potatoes and add in the fish; cook until the fish is crispy, 12-14 minutes. Serve.

Nutrition: Calories:233; fat: 15g; Carbohydrates: 28g; Protein: 25g

20. Smoked Salmon Taquitos

Preparation time: 5 minutes

Cooking time: 10 minutes

Servings: 4

Ingredients:

- 2 tablespoon. olive oil

- 1 lb. smoked salmon, chopped

- Salt to taste

- 2 tablespoon. taco seasoning

- 1 cup cheddar cheese

- 1 lime, juiced

- ½ cup fresh cilantro, chopped

- 8 corn tortillas

Directions:

1. Preheat air fryer to 390 F. In a bowl, mix salmon, taco seasoning, lime juice, cheddar cheese, salt, and cilantro.

2. Divide the mixture between the tortillas. Wrap the tortillas around the filling and place them in the greased air fryer basket.

3. Bake for 10 minutes, turning once halfway through. Serve with hot salsa.

Nutrition: Calories: 345; fat: 10g; Carbohydrates: 19g; Protein: 32g

POULTRY RECIPES

21. Crispy Southern Fried Chicken

Preparation time: 10 minutes

Cooking time: 25 minutes

Servings: 4

Ingredients:

- teaspoon. cayenne pepper

- 2 tablespoon. mustard powder

- 2 tablespoon. oregano

- 2 tablespoon. thyme

- 3 tablespoon. coconut milk

- 1 beaten egg

- ¼ C. cauliflower

- ¼ C. gluten-free oats

- 8 chicken drumsticks

Directions:

1. Ensure air fryer is preheated to 350 degrees.

2. Lay out chicken and season with pepper and salt on all sides.

3. Add all other ingredients to a blender, blending till a smooth-like breadcrumb mixture is created. Place in a bowl and add a beaten egg to another bowl.

4. Dip chicken into breadcrumbs, then into egg, and breadcrumbs once more.

5. Place coated drumsticks into air fryer and cook 20 minutes. Bump up the temperature to 390 degrees and cook another 5 minutes till crispy.

Nutrition: Calories: 504 Fat: 18g Protein: 35g Sugar: 5g

22. Air Fryer Turkey Breast

Preparation time: 5 minutes

Cooking time: 60 minutes

Servings: 8

Ingredients:

- Pepper and salt

- 1 oven-ready turkey breast

- Turkey seasonings of choice

Directions:

1. Preheat air fryer to 350 degrees.

2. Season turkey with pepper, salt, and other desired seasonings.

3. Place turkey in air fryer basket.

4. Cook 60 minutes. The meat should be at 165 degrees when done.

5. Allow to rest 10-15 minutes before slicing. Enjoy!

Nutrition: Calories: 212 Fat: 12g Protein: 24g Sugar: 0g

MEAT RECIPES

23. Beef Taco Roll-Ups with Cotija Cheese

Preparation time: 10 minutes

Cooking time: 15 minutes

Servings: 4

Ingredients:

- 1 tablespoon sesame oil

- 2 tablespoons scallions, chopped

- 1 garlic clove, minced

- 1 bell pepper, chopped

- 1/2-pound ground beef

- 1/2 teaspoon Mexican oregano

- 1/2 teaspoon dried marjoram

- 1 teaspoon chili powder

- 1/2 cup refried beans

- Sea salt and ground black pepper, to taste

- 1/2 cup Cotija cheese, shredded

- 8 roll wrappers

Directions:

1. Start by preheating your Air Fryer to 395 degrees F.

2. Heat the sesame oil in a nonstick skillet over medium-high heat. Cook the scallions, garlic, and peppers until tender and fragrant.

3. Add the ground beef, oregano, marjoram, and chili powder. Continue cooking for 3 minutes longer or until it is browned.

4. Stir in the beans, salt, and pepper. Divide the meat/bean mixture between wrappers that are softened with a little bit of water. Top with cheese.

5. Roll the wrappers and spritz them with cooking oil on all sides.

6. Cook in the preheated Air Fryer for 11 to 12 minutes, flipping them halfway through the cooking time. Enjoy!

Nutrition: 417 Calories; 15.9g Fat; 41g Carbs; 26.2g Protein; 1.5g Sugars

24. Barbecue Skirt Steak

Preparation time: 8 minutes

Cooking time: 12 minutes

Servings: 5

Ingredients:

- 2 pounds' skirt steak

- 2 tablespoons tomato paste

- 1 tablespoon tomato ketchup

- 1 tablespoon olive oil

- 1 tablespoon soy sauce

- 1/4 cup rice vinegar

- 1 tablespoon fish sauce

- Sea salt, to taste

- 1/2 teaspoon dried dill

- 1/2 teaspoon dried rosemary

- 1/4 teaspoon black pepper, freshly cracked

- 1 tablespoon brown sugar

Directions:

1. Place all ingredients in a large ceramic dish; let it marinate for 3 hours in your refrigerator.

2. Coat the sides and bottom of the Air Fryer with cooking spray.

3. Add your steak to the cooking basket; reserve the marinade. Cook the skirt steak in the preheated Air Fryer at 400 degrees F for 12 minutes, turning over a couple of times, basting with the reserved marinade.

4. Serve warm with roasted new potatoes, if desired.

Nutrition: 394 Calories; 19g Fat; 4.4g Carbs; 51.3g Protein; 3.3g Sugars

25. Kid-Friendly Mini Meatloaves

Preparation time: 5 minutes

Cooking time: 25 minutes

Servings: 4

Ingredients:

- 2 tablespoons bacon, chopped

- 1 small-sized onion, chopped

- 1 bell pepper, chopped

- 1 garlic clove, minced

- 1-pound ground beef

- 1/2 teaspoon dried basil

- 1/2 teaspoon dried mustard seeds

- 1/2 teaspoon dried marjoram

- Salt and black pepper, to taste

- 1/2 cup panko crumbs

- 4 tablespoons tomato puree

Directions:

1. Heat a nonstick skillet over medium-high heat; cook the bacon for 1 to 2 minutes; add the onion, bell pepper, and garlic and cook another 3 minutes or until fragrant.

2. Heat off. Stir in the ground beef, spices, and panko crumbs. Stir until well combined. Shape the mixture into four mini meatloaves.

3. Preheat your Air Fryer to 350 degrees F. Spritz the cooking basket with nonstick spray.

4. Place the mini meatloaves in the cooking basket and cook for 10 minutes; turn them over, top with the tomato puree and continue to cook for 10 minutes more. Bon appétit!

Nutrition: 451 Calories; 27.6g Fat; 15.3g Carbs; 33.4g Protein; 3.7g Sugars

26. Quick Sausage and Veggie Sandwiches

Preparation time: 5 minutes

Cooking time: 30 minutes

Servings: 4

Ingredients:

- 4 bell peppers

- 2 tablespoons canola oil

- 4 medium-sized tomatoes, halved

- 4 spring onions

- 4 beef sausages

- 4 hot dog buns

- 1 tablespoon mustard

Directions:

Start by preheating your Air Fryer to 400 degrees F.

1. Add the bell peppers to the cooking basket. Drizzle 1 tablespoon of canola oil all over the bell peppers.

2. Cook for 5 minutes. Turn the temperature down to 350 degrees F. Add the tomatoes and spring onions to the cooking basket and cook an additional 10 minutes.

3. Reserve your vegetables.

4. Then, add the sausages to the cooking basket. Drizzle with the remaining tablespoon of canola oil.

5. Cook in the preheated Air Fryer at 380 degrees F for 15 minutes, flipping them halfway through the cooking time.

6. Add the sausage to a hot dog bun; top with the air-fried vegetables and mustard; serve.

Nutrition: 627 Calories; 41.9g Fat; 41.3g Carbs; 22.2g Protein; 9.3g Sugars

27. Mayonnaise and Rosemary Grilled Steak

Preparation time: 5 minutes

Cooking time: 15 minutes

Servings: 4

Ingredients:

- 1 cup mayonnaise

- 1 tablespoon fresh rosemary, finely chopped

- 2 tablespoons Worcestershire sauce

- Sea salt, to taste

- 1/2 teaspoon ground black pepper

- 1 teaspoon smoked paprika

- 1 teaspoon garlic, minced

- 1 ½ pounds short loin steak

Directions:

1. Combine the mayonnaise, rosemary, Worcestershire sauce, salt, pepper, paprika, and garlic; mix to combine well.

2. Now, brush the mayonnaise mixture over both sides of the steak. Lower the steak onto the grill pan.

3. Grill in the preheated Air Fryer at 390 degrees F for 8 minutes. Turn the steaks over and grill an additional 7 minutes.

4. Check for doneness with a meat thermometer. Serve warm and enjoy!

Nutrition: 620 Calories; 50g Fat; 2.8g Carbs; 39.7g Protein; 1.3g Sugars

VEGETABLE RECIPES

28. Apple Cider Donuts

Preparation Time: 25 minutes

Cooking Time: 45 minutes

Servings: 14

Ingredients:

For the donuts:

- 2 Cups of apple cider

- All-purpose flour: 3 cups

- Medium brown sugar: ½ cup

- Baking powder: 2 teaspoons

- Ground cinnamon: 1 teaspoon

- Ground ginger: 1 teaspoon

- Baking soda: ½ teaspoon

- Kosher salt: ½ teaspoon

- 8 Tablespoons of cold unsalted butter (1 stick)

- 1/2 cup frozen milk

For finishing and shaping:

1. All-purpose flour: ¼ cup

2. Unsalted butter: 8 tablespoons

3. Granulated sugar: 1 cup

4. 1 Teaspoon cinnamon

Direction:

1. Dough **preparation time:** Pour 2 cups of apple cider into a small saucepan over medium-high heat and bring to a boil. Boil until half (to 1 cup) is reduced, for 10 to 12 minutes.

2. Error on the over-reducing side (you can always add a bit of extra apple cider to the reduced amount).

3. Move the cider reduction to a measuring cup that is heatproof and cool fully, about 30 minutes.

4. In a wide bowl, put 3 cups of all-purpose flour, 1/2 cup of light brown powdered sugar, 1 teaspoon of crushed cinnamon, 1 teaspoon of ground ginger, 2 teaspoons of baking powder, 1/2 teaspoon of kosher salt and 1/2 teaspoon of baking soda to mix.

5. Grate 8 tablespoons of cold unsalted butter on a grater's large holes. Add the grated butter to the flour mixture and

melt the butter with your fingers until it is about the size of tiny pebbles.

6. Create a well in the center of the mixture. Add the 1 cup reduced cider and 1/2 cup cold milk to the well and mix the dough using a large spatula.

7. Shaping the dough:

8. Sprinkle a few spoonsful of flour on a work surface. Put the batter on the floor. Pat the dough with a rolling pin into an even layer about 1-inch-thick, then add more flour with it.

9. Fold on the dough and pat it down until 1-inch thick. Again fold and pat, repeat the process six times, until the dough is slightly springy. Pat the dough into a 9x13-inch rough rectangle about 1/2 inch thick.

10. Cut donuts with a floured donut cutter (or 3 inches and 1 inch round cutter) out of the dough. From the first round of cutting, you will be getting around 8 donuts. Place the doughnuts onto a butter paper.

11. Collect the scraps, pat the dough down again and repeat cutting until approximately 18 donuts are in place.

Refrigerate the donuts for about 10 minutes, while preheating the air fryer to 375°F.

12. Prepare the coating:

13. Melt and put the remaining 8 tablespoons of butter in a medium dish. In a small bowl, place 1 cup of granulated sugar and 1 teaspoon of ground cinnamon, and whisk with a fork.

14. Cooking: Air fry in groups of 3 to 4 at a time, flipping them halfway through, 12 minutes per group, depending on the size of your air fryer; switch the donuts to a wire rack and load the next batch onto the air fryer.

15. In the meantime, first, dip the fried doughnuts in the butter and then cinnamon sugar. Place the wire rack back in. For dipping, serve the donuts warm or at room temperature with the dipping of hot cider.

Nutrition: Calories: 318 Fat: 12.4 g Saturated Fat: 7.7 g Carbs: 49.1 g Fiber: 1.1 g Sugars: 25.8 g Protein: 3.5 g Sodium: 173.8 mg

29. Mini Apple Pies

Preparation Time: 30 Minutes

Cooking: 15 Minutes

Servings: 4

Ingredients:

- Butter: 4 tablespoons

- Brown sugar: 6 tablespoons

- Ground cinnamon: 1 teaspoon

- Granny smith apples: 2 medium sized and diced

- Cornstarch: 1 teaspoon

- Cold water: 2 teaspoons

- 1/2 (14 ounces) 9-inch double-crust pastry pack

- Cooking spray

- Grapeseed oil: ½ tablespoon

- Powdered sugar: ¼ cup

- 1 teaspoon of milk, or more if required

Directions:

1. In a nonstick skillet, combine the apples, butter, brown sugar, and cinnamon. Cook over a normal heat for about 6 minutes, until apples have softened.

2. Take cold water and dissolves cornstarch in it. Stir in apple mixture and cook for about 1 minute, until sauce thickens. Remove from heat the apple pie filling and set aside to cool while the crust is being prepared.

3. Put the pie crust on a lightly floured surface and slightly roll out to smooth the dough surface. Cut the dough into small enough rectangles to allow 2 to fit in your air fryer at once. Repeat with the remainder of the crust until you have 8 equal rectangles, re-rolling some of the dough scraps if necessary.

4. Wet the outer corners of 4 rectangles with water, and place some apple filling around 1/2 inch from the edges in the center.

5. Roll the remaining 4 rectangles out, so they're slightly larger than the ones filled. Place those rectangles on top of the fill; crimp the edges with a fork. Cut 4 tiny slits into the heads of the pies.

6. Grease an air fryer basket with cooking spray. Use a spatula to brush the tops of 2 pies with grapeseed oil and transfer pastries to the air fryer basket.

7. Insert a basket and set the temperature to 385 °F (195 °C). Bake for about 8 minutes, until golden brown.

8. Remove the pies from the basket and repeat with the 2 pies that are remaining.

9. Take a small bowl and add the powdered sugar and milk in it. Brush the glaze and allow it to dry on warm pies. Serve the pies warm.

Nutrition: Calories 498 | Fat 28.6 g Cholesterol 31 mg Sodium 328 mg Carbohydrates 59.8 g Protein 3.3 g

30. Air Fryer Glazed Cake Doughnut Holes

Preparation Time: 25 Minutes

Cooking Time: 35 Minutes

Servings: 14

Ingredients:

- All-purpose flour: 1 ¼ cups (approx. 5 3/8 oz.), plus more for working surfaces

- Granulated sugar: 1 tablespoon

- Baking powder: 1 teaspoon

- Table salt: ¼ teaspoon

- Cold salted butter: 4 tablespoons, cut into small cubes

- Whole milk: 1/3 cup

- Cooking spray

- 1 cup of powdered sugar (approx. 8 oz.)

- Water: 3 tablespoons

Directions:

1. In a medium bowl, whisk the flour, sugar, baking powder, and salt together. Add butter; use 2 knives or a pastry cutter

to cut into flour until the butter is well mixed and looks like coarse cornmeal.

2. Add milk, and stir until the ball forms a dough.

3. Place the dough on a floured surface and knead for about 30 seconds until the dough is smooth, forming a cohesive disk. Cut the dough into 14 identical balls. Gently roll each to form even smooth balls.

4. Coat the air fryer basket bottom thoroughly with a cooking spray. Place 7 dough balls in the air fryer tray, spaced uniformly so as not to hit. Spray cooking spray on dough balls.

5. Cook for about 10 minutes, at 350 ° F until browned and puffed. Remove gently from the basket, and put on a rack of wire.

6. Whisk the caster sugar and water together until smooth in a medium cup. Place the cooked dough balls in glaze, 1 at a time; roll to coat.

7. Put to dry on a wire rack or baking sheet lined with parchment paper.

8. Repeat procedure with dough and glaze remaining.

9. Serve warm.

Nutrition: Calories: 330 Fat: 17.5 g Saturated: 8.5 g Carbs: 42.9 g

Fiber: 1.9 g Sugars: 28.0 g Protein: 4.0 g Sodium: 172.1 mg

31. Air Fryer Cinnamon Sugar Churros

Preparation Time: 60 Minutes

Cooking time: 10 minutes

Servings: 26

Ingredients:

The Churros:

- Water: 1 cup

- Butter: ½ cup

- Granulated sugar: 1 tablespoon

- All-purpose flour: 1 cup

- Eggs: 3

- Vanilla extract: ½ teaspoon

- 1/2 cup of granulated sucrose

- Cinnamon: 2 teaspoons

For Chocolate Sauce:

1. Chocolate chips: ¾ cup

2. Coconut oil: 1 tablespoon

Directions:

1. Boil water in a saucepan on the burner and add in 1 tablespoon of sugar and butter.

2. Reduce heat to medium/low once melted, and fold in the flour. Take off fire.

3. Whisk the eggs and the vanilla extract together in a separate bowl.

4. Little by little, insert some eggs into the dough. Continue to repeat until eggs are well mixed into the dough. Let's let it cool.

5. Place dough with a star-shaped tip inside a pastry bag. Pipe 6-inch long churros on a baking pan or silicone mat lined with a parchment paper.

6. Place the tray in the fridge for 35 minutes to chill. (This makes the dough stickier and simpler to deal with.)

7. Place a single layer of churros in the air fryer, and do not touch each other—Air-fry at 380 degrees for 10 minutes.

8. Mix 1/2 cup of sugar and the cinnamon on a small plate.

9. Once the churros have been cooked, roll them in the mixture of cinnamon sugar and place them on a cookie cooling rack. Repeat this until all of the churros are fried.

10. Melt chocolate chips and coconut oil in a glass bowl for about 20-30 seconds, using the microwave to make the chocolate sauce. Mix well, then dip warm churros in the serving sauce!

Nutrition: Calories 289 Protein 32 Carbs 17 Fats 8

32. Air Fryer Brownies

Preparation Time: 5 Minutes

Cooking Time: 30 minutes

Servings: 2

Ingredients:

- Granulated sugar: ½ cup

- Cocoa Powder: 1/3 cup

- All-purpose flour: ¼ cup

- Baking powder: ¼ teaspoon

- A pinch of kosher salt

- Butter: ¼ cup melted and gently cooled

- 1 Big Egg

Directions:

1. Grease a 7 "round cake pan with cooking spray. Mix together sugar, cocoa powder, flour, baking powder, and salt in a medium bowl.

2. Whisk butter and egg until combined in a small bowl. Mix dry ingredients to wet ingredients and stir until combined.

3. Transfer brownie batter to the greasy cake pan and smooth top. Cook for 16-18 minutes in the air fryer at 350 °. Let it cool for 10 minutes before slicing.

Nutrition: Calories 389 Protein 22 Carbs 16 Fats 9

33. Strawberry Cheesecake Chimichanga

Preparation time: 20 minutes

Cooking time: 10 minutes

Servings: 6

Ingredients:

- Cream cheese: 1 package kept at room temperature

- Sour cream: ¼ cup

- Sugar: ¼ cup plus 1 tablespoon

- Vanilla extract: 1 teaspoon

- Lemon zest: ½ teaspoon

- Soft flour tortillas: 6 (8-inch)

- 1 3/4 cups of sliced strawberries

- Cinnamon: 1 tablespoon

Directions:

1. Beat the sour cream with the cream cheese, 1 tablespoon of sugar, vanilla extract, and lemon zest in the container of an electric mixer fitted with the paddle attachment, scraping down the sides of the bowl as desired.

2. Fold up the sliced strawberries in 3/4 cup.

3. If you warm them up a little bit in the microwave, the tortillas can bend easier. Leave them in the kit and spend 30-45 seconds in.

4. Divide the mixture evenly between the tortillas, slathering each portion of each tortilla in the bottom third.

5. Then turn the two sides of each tortilla towards the middle and roll up the tortilla like a burrito, and protect it with a toothpick. The remaining tortillas replicate the rolling process. Take a deep bowl, and add the remaining 1/4 cup sugar with the cinnamon and set them aside. Set the air fryer at 400 degrees. Place the chimichangas in the basket of an air fryer. Spray some cooking spray over the chimichanga.

6. Set the timer within 6 minutes.

7. Take out chimichangas from the basket after 6 minutes.

8. Roll them out into the mixture of cinnamon and sugar.

9. Remove the chimichangas from all the toothpicks and place them on the serving plates.

10. Cover each slice of strawberries with chimichanga and serve immediately.

Nutrition: Calories 249 Protein 12 Carbs 37 Fats 3

34. Peanut Butter Cookies

Preparation time: 2 minutes

Cooking time: 5 minutes

Servings:1

Ingredients:

- Peanut Butter: 1 cup

- Sugar: 1 cup

- 1 Egg

Directions:

1. Mix all the ingredients with a hand mixer. Spray trays of air fryer with canola oil. (Alternatively, parchment paper can also be used, but it will take longer to cook your cookies) Set the air fryer temperature to 350 degrees and preheat it. Place rounded dough balls onto air fryer trays. Press gently down with the back of a fork. Place air fryer tray in your air fryer in the middle place. Cook for five minutes.

2. Use milk to serve with cookies.

Nutrition: Calories: 236 Fat: 13g Saturated fat: 3g Cholesterol: 19mg Sodium: 130mg Carbohydrates: 26g Fiber: 1g Sugar: 22g Protein: 6g

35. Banana Muffins

Preparation time: 10 minutes

Cooking time: 10 Minutes

Servings: 10

Ingredients:

- 2 very ripe, peeled bananas

- 1 medium-size egg

- 1/2 cup brown sugar

- 1/3 cup olive oil

- 1 teaspoon of vanilla extract

- ¾ cup self-rising flour

- 1 teaspoon of cinnamon

Directions:

1. Preheat the air fryer to 320 degrees F for 5 minutes.

2. Add the bananas to a bowl, and mash.

3. Next, to the mashed bananas, add the egg, brown sugar, oil, and vanilla. Stir thoroughly to combine.

4. Sprinkle the flour and cinnamon over the top and fold until combined.

5. Evenly divide the mixture between 10 muffin cases and place them in the air fryer basket.

6. Place the basket in the air fryer and bake until golden and springy to the touch, for 15 minutes. You may need to do this in batches.

7. Transfer the muffins to a wire baking rack and allow the muffins to cool completely while in their cases.

Nutrition: Calories: 285 Total Fat: 5.1g Total carbs: 32.2g

36. Banana Boat S'mores

Preparation time: 10 minutes

Cooking time: 15 Minutes

Servings: 4

Ingredients:

- 4 ripe bananas

- 3 tablespoons of semisweet chocolate chips

- 3 tablespoons of peanut butter chips

- 3 tablespoons of miniature marshmallows

- 3 tablespoons of graham cracker cereal

Directions:

1. Preheat the air fryer to 400 degrees F.

2. Using a knife, slice each banana down the center from one end to the other but do not cut all the way through the banana.

3. Gently open the incision to create a pocket for fillings.

4. Fill the pocket with your desired amount and combination of choc chips, peanut butter chips, mini marshmallows, and graham cracker cereal.

5. Place the bananas in the air fryer basket, set them side by side so that they stand up.

6. Cook in the air fryer for approximately 6 minutes or until the banana peel has blackened, and the fillings have started to melt.

7. Take the bananas out of the air fryer and allow it to cool for 3-4 minutes before serving.

Nutrition: Calories: 185 Total Fat: 6.1g Total carbs: 22.2g

37. Brazilian Grilled Pineapple

Preparation time: 10 minutes

Cooking time: 20 Minutes

Servings: 4

Ingredients:

- 1 whole peeled and cored pineapple

- 2 teaspoons of ground cinnamon

- ½ cup of brown sugar

- 3 tablespoons of melted butter

Directions:

1. Cut the pineapple into spears.

2. In a small bowl, combine the cinnamon and sugar.

3. Brush the pineapple spears all over with melted butter and sprinkle over the sugar-cinnamon. Pat the sugar gently to ensure it has adhered.

4. Arrange the pineapple in a single layer in the air fryer basket; you may need to do this in batches.

5. Cook the pineapple for 8-10 minutes at 400 degrees F. Halfway through the cooking time, flip the pineapple and brush with a little more butter.

6. Take the pineapple out of the air fryer and serve.

Nutrition: Calories: 409 Total Fat: 5.5g Total carbs: 22g

FAST FOOD

38. Pizza with Salami and Mushrooms

Preparation time: 15 minutes

Cooking time: 30 minutes

Servings: 1

Ingredients:

- 4 oz. flour

- 1 teaspoon instant yeast

- Salt to taste ½ tablespoon. olive oil

- 2 oz. tomato sauce

- ½ ball of mozzarella, sliced thinly

- 2-3 mushrooms, sliced

- 2 oz. salami, in strips

- 2 teaspoon dried oregano

- 2 tablespoon. Parmesan cheese, grated

- Freshly ground black pepper

- Handful of arugula

- Small pizza pan, 7 - inch diameter, buttered

Directions:

1. Combine the flour and yeast with a pinch of salt, water (2-3 oz.), and olive oil. Mix to form a smooth dough ball, and knead until you have an elastic and flexible dough.

2. Ensure that your air fryer is preheated to 390 F.

3. Flour your work surface, and on it, roll out the dough to a 7 - inch round, and put the same in the pizza pan. Form a crust by folding the excess edge of the dough inward.

4. Spread the tomato sauce evenly over the dough, and on top of the sauce, add the mozzarella slices.

5. Ensure even distribution of the mushrooms and the salami over the cheese. Add some sprinkles of oregano, Parmesan cheese, pepper, and arugula on the pizza.

6. Transfer the pizza pan into the air fryer basket, and bake the pizza until golden brown - it takes about 12 minutes.

7. You may use ready-to-use pizza dough for faster but same results.

Nutrition: calories 463, fat 11, fiber 14, carbs 20, protein 22

39. Simple Grilled American Cheese Sandwich

Preparation time: 5 minutes

Cooking time: 8 minutes

Servings: 1

Ingredients:

- 2-3 slices cheddar cheese

- 2 slices sandwich bread

- 2 teaspoon Butter

Directions:

1. With the cheese between the bread slices, spread the butter to the outside of both slices of bread.

2. Transfer the buttered bread into the air fryer and allow to cook for 8 minutes at 370 F.

3. After 4 minutes, flip the bread, and allow to cook for the next 4 minutes.

4. Note that you can use any type of cheese you want and may stuff with tomatoes if that's your preference.

Nutrition: calories 523, fat 6.9, fiber 2.8, carbs 5.9, protein 15

SALAD RECIPES

40. Cauliflower Salad

Preparation time: 20 minutes

Cooking Time: 10 minutes

Servings: 4

Ingredients:

- For Salad

- ¼ cup golden raisins

- 1 cup boiling water

- ¼ cup olive oil

- 1 head cauliflower, cut into small florets

- 1 tablespoon curry powder

- Salt, to taste

- ¼ cup pecans, toasted and chopped

- 2 tablespoons fresh mint leaves, chopped

- For Dressing:

- 1 cup mayonnaise

- 2 tablespoons sugar

- 1 tablespoon fresh lemon juice

Directions:

1. For salad: in a bowl, add the cauliflower, curry powder, salt, and oil and toss to coat well.

2. Set the temperature of air fryer to 390 degrees F. Grease an air fryer basket.

3. Arrange cauliflower florets into the prepared air fryer basket in a single layer.

4. Air fry for about 8-10 minutes.

5. Meanwhile, in a bowl, add the raisins, and boiling water and set aside until using.

6. Remove from air fryer and transfer the cauliflower florets onto a plate.

7. Set aside to cool.

8. Drain the raisins well.

9. For dressing: in a bowl, add all the ingredients and mix until well combined.

10. In another bowl, mix together the cauliflower, raisins and pecans.

11. Add the dressing and gently, stir to combine.

12. Refrigerate to chill before serving.

13. Garnish with mint and serve

Nutrition: Calories: 162 Carbohydrate: 25.3g Protein: 11.3g Fat: 3.1g Sugar: 1.6g Sodium: 160mg

SNACK & APPETIZERS RECIPES

41. Chicken Vegetable Nuggets

Preparation time: 10 minutes.

Cooking Time: 10 minutes.

Servings: 6

Ingredients:

- ½ of zucchini, roughly chopped

- ½ of carrot, roughly chopped

- 14 oz. chicken breast, cut into chunks

- ½ tablespoon mustard powder

- 1 tablespoon garlic powder

- 1 tablespoon onion powder

- Salt and black pepper, to taste

- 1 cup all-purpose flour

- 2 tablespoons milk

- 1 egg

- 1 cup panko breadcrumbs

Directions:

1. In a food processor, add the zucchini and carrot and pulse until finely chopped.

2. Add the chicken, mustard powder, garlic powder, onion powder, salt, and black pepper and pulse until well combined. In a shallow dish, place the flour. In a second dish, mix together the milk and egg.

3. In a third dish, put the breadcrumbs. Coat the chicken vegetable nuggets with flour, then dip into the egg mixture, and finally, coat with the breadcrumbs.

4. Arrange the nuggets in Air Fryer Basket inside the Instant Pot. Put on the Instant Air Fryer lid and cook on Air Fry mode for 10 minutes at 400 degrees F. Once done, remove the lid and serve warm.

Nutrition: calories: 81 Protein: 0.4g Carbs: 4.7g Fat: 8.3g

42. Crusted Cod Nuggets

Preparation time: 10 minutes.

Cooking Time: 8 minutes.

Servings: 6

Ingredients:

- 1 cup all-purpose flour

- 2 eggs

- ¾ cup breadcrumbs

- Pinch of salt

- 2 tablespoons olive oil

- 1 lb. cod, cut into 1½inch strips

Directions:

1. In a shallow dish, place the flour. Crack the eggs in a second dish and beat well. In a third dish, mix together the breadcrumbs, salt, and oil.

2. Coat the cod nuggets with flour, then dip into beaten eggs and finally, coat with the breadcrumbs.

3. Arrange the nuggets in Air Fryer Basket inside the Instant Pot. Put on the Instant Air Fryer lid and cook on Air Fry mode for 8 minutes at 380 degrees F.

4. Once done, remove the lid and serve warm.

Nutrition: calories: 134 Protein: 2.1g Carbs: 24.3g Fat: 5g

43. Nutty Air Fried Turnips

Preparation time: 20 minutes

Cooking time: 1 hour

Servings:

Ingredients:

- 2 large turnips, scrubbed

- 1 tablespoon extra-virgin olive oil

- 1 tablespoon macadamia nut oil

- 1/2 teaspoon coarse sea salt

- 1/2 teaspoon ground peppercorns

Directions:

1. Preheat your air fryer to 400 degrees F

2. Brush potatoes with oil and sprinkle with the rest of the ingredients.

3. Place in an air fryer basket and cook for 1 hour or until fork tender.

Nutrition: Calories: 180, Total Fat: 12g, Carbs: 22g, Protein: 34g

44. Air Fried Parsnips in Hazelnut Oil

Preparation time: minutes

Cooking time: 1 hour

Servings: 4

Ingredients:

- 2 large parsnips, scrubbed

- 1 tablespoon hazelnut oil

- 1/2 teaspoon coarse sea salt

Directions:

1. Preheat your air fryer to 400 degrees F

2. Brush potatoes with oil and sprinkle with the rest of the ingredients.

3. Place in an air fryer basket and cook for 1 hour or until fork tender.

Nutrition: Calories: 240, Total Fat: 4g, Carbs: 13g, Protein: 34g

45. Air Fried Potatoes in Hazelnut Oil

Preparation time: 20 minutes

Cooking time: 60 minutes

Servings: 2

Ingredients:

- 2 large russet potatoes, scrubbed

- 1 tablespoon hazelnut oil

- 1/2 teaspoon coarse sea salt

- 1/2 teaspoon coarse black pepper

Directions:

1. Preheat your air fryer to 400 degrees F

2. Brush potatoes with oil and sprinkle with the rest of the ingredients.

3. Place in an air fryer basket and cook for 1 hour or until fork tender.

Nutrition: Calories: 470, Total Fat: 9g, Carbs: 15g, Protein: 44g

46. Air Fried Brussels Sprouts with Bacon and Balsamic Vinegar

Preparation time: 25 minutes

Cooking time: 10 minutes

Servings: 3

Ingredients:

- 10 ounces Brussels sprouts, trimmed and halved lengthwise

- Garnishing Ingredients

- 1 teaspoon balsamic vinegar

- 2 teaspoons crumbled cooked bacon (optional)

- Seasoning Ingredients

- 1 teaspoon olive oil

- 1/2 teaspoon sea salt

- 1/2 teaspoon ground black pepper

Directions:

1. Preheat your air fryer to 350 degrees F.

2. Combine the seasoning ingredients thoroughly.

3. Add the vegetables and toss to coat.

4. Place in the basket of the air fryer and fry for 5 minutes

5. Shake and cook for another 5 minutes

6. Sprinkle with garnishing ingredients.

Nutrition: Calories: 178, Total Fat: 7g, Carbs: 18g, Protein: 12g

47. Air Fried Broccoli Florets with Almonds and Sea Salt

Preparation time: 10 minutes

Cooking time: 10 minutes

Servings: 5

Ingredients:

- 10 ounces' broccoli florets, trimmed and halved lengthwise

- Garnishing Ingredients

- 1 teaspoon sesame oil

- 2 teaspoons crumbled dried seaweed or crushed almonds

- 1/2 teaspoon. sea salt

- Seasoning Ingredients

- 1 teaspoon sesame oil

- 1/2 teaspoon salt

- 1/2 teaspoon ground black pepper

Directions:

1. Preheat your air fryer to 350 degrees F.

2. Combine the seasoning ingredients thoroughly.

3. Add the vegetables and toss to coat.

4. Place in the basket of the air fryer and fry for 5 minutes

5. Shake and cook for another 5 minutes

6. Sprinkle with garnishing ingredients.

Nutrition: Calories: 567, Total Fat: 16g, Carbs: 21g, Protein: 23g

48. Cauliflower with Cayenne Pepper and Pancetta

Preparation time: 10 minutes

Cooking time: 10 minutes **Servings:** 4

Ingredients:

- 10 ounces' cauliflower, trimmed and halved lengthwise

- Garnishing Ingredients

- 1/2 teaspoon cayenne pepper

- 2 teaspoons crumbled cooked pancetta (optional)

- Seasoning Ingredients

- 1 teaspoon olive oil

- 1/2 teaspoon salt

- 1/2 teaspoon ground black pepper

Directions:

1. Preheat your air fryer to 350 degrees F. Combine the seasoning ingredients thoroughly. Add the vegetables and toss to coat. Place in the basket of the air fryer and fry for 5 minutesShake and cook for another 5 minutesSprinkle with garnishing ingredients.

Nutrition: Calories: 560, Total Fat: 8g, Carbs: 17g, Protein: 33g

49. Smoky Air Fried Asparagus with Sesame Seeds

Preparation time: 5 minutes

Cooking time: 10 minutes

Servings: 3

Ingredients:

- 8 ounces Asparagus spears, trimmed and halved crosswise

- Garnishing Ingredients

- 1 teaspoon smoked paprika

- 2 teaspoons sesame seeds

- Seasoning Ingredients

- 1 teaspoon peanut oil

- 1/2 teaspoon salt

- 1/2 teaspoon ground black pepper

Directions:

1. Preheat your air fryer to 350 degrees F.

2. Combine the seasoning ingredients thoroughly.

3. Add the vegetables and toss to coat.

4. Place in the basket of the air fryer and fry for 5 minutes

5. Shake and cook for another 5 minutes

6. Sprinkle with garnishing ingredients.

Nutrition: Calories: 330 Fat: 17.5 g Saturated: 8.5 g Carbs: 42.9 g

Fiber: 1.9 g Sugars: 28.0 g Protein: 4.0 g Sodium: 172.1 mg

50. Mini Cabbages with Pancetta and Rainbow

Peppercorns

Preparation time: 5 minutes

Cooking time: 10 minutes

Servings: 2

Ingredients:

- 10 ounces' mini cabbages, trimmed and halved lengthwise

- Garnishing Ingredients

- 1 teaspoon extra virgin olive oil

- 2 teaspoons crumbled cooked pancetta (optional)

- Seasoning Ingredients

- 1 teaspoon extra virgin oil

- 1/2 teaspoon salt

- 1/2 teaspoon rainbow peppercorns

Directions:

1. Preheat your air fryer to 350 degrees F.

2. Combine the seasoning ingredients thoroughly.

3. Add the vegetables and toss to coat.

4. Place in the basket of the air fryer and fry for 5 minutes

5. Shake and cook for another 5 minutes

6. Sprinkle with garnishing ingredients.

Nutrition: Calories: 730, Total Fat: 21g, Carbs: 11g, Protein: 19g

30 DAYS MEAL PLAN

Days	Breakfast	Snacks	Dinner
1	Sausage and Egg Breakfast Burrito	Eggplant Mix	Roasted Salmon with Lemon and Rosemary
2	Eggs in Avocado	Garlic Kale	Air Fried Meatballs with Parsley
3	French Toast Sticks	Herbed Tomatoes	Succulent Flank Steak
4	Home-Fried Potatoes	Coriander Potatoes	Chili Roasted Eggplant Soba
5	Homemade Cherry Breakfast Tarts	Tomatoes and Green beans	Quinoa and Spinach Cakes
6	Sausage and Cream Cheese Biscuits	Buttery Artichokes	Air Fried Cajun Shrimp
7	Fried Chicken and Waffles	Ginger Mushrooms	Air Fried Squid Rings
8	Cheesy Tater Tot Breakfast Bake	Masala Potatoes	Marinated Portobello Mushroom
9	Breakfast Scramble Casserole	Mixed Veggie Chips	Air Fried Meatloaf
10	Homemade Cherry Breakfast Tarts	Pear and Apple Chips	Fettuccini with Roasted Vegetables in Tomato Sauce
11	Mozzarella Tots	Banana and Cocoa Chips	Herbed Parmesan Turkey Meatballs
12	Chicken Balls	Roasted Chickpeas	Teriyaki Glazed Salmon and Vegetable Roast
13	Tofu Egg Scramble	Zucchini Chips	Sirloin with Garlic and Thyme
14	Flax & Hemp Porridge	Ranch Garlic Pretzels	Herbed Parmesan Turkey Meatballs

15	Creamy Bacon Eggs	Yellow Squash and Cream Cheese Fritters	Yogurt Garlic Chicken
16	Cheddar Bacon Hash	Air Fry Cheesy Taco Hot dogs	Lemony Parmesan Salmon
17	Cheddar Soufflé with Herbs	Crispy French Toast Sticks	Easiest Tuna Cobbler Ever
18	Bacon Butter Biscuits	Buttered Corn Cob	Deliciously Homemade Pork Buns
19	Keto Parmesan Frittata	Roasted Cashews	Mouthwatering Tuna Melts
20	Chicken Liver Pate	Panko Zucchini Fries	Bacon Wings
21	Coconut Pancake Hash	Rosemary Turnip Chips	Pepper Pesto Lamb
22	Beef Slices	Rosemary Carrot Fries	Tuna Spinach Casserole
23	Flax & Chia Porridge	Butternut Squash Fries	Greek Style Mini Burger Pies
24	Paprika Eggs with Bacon	Breaded Pickle Fries	Family Fun Pizza
25	Quiche Muffin Cups	Buttered Corn Cob	Crispy Hot Sauce Chicken
26	Easy Scotch Eggs	Polenta Bars	Herbed Parmesan Turkey Meatballs
27	Strawberry Toast	Eggplant Crisps	Sweet Potatoes & Creamy Crisp Chicken
28	Cinnamon Sweet-Potato Chips	Roasted Pecans	Mushroom & Chicken Noodles with Glasswort and Sesame
29	Quiche Muffin Cups	Crispy Broccoli Poppers	Prawn Chicken Drumettes
30	Vegetable and Ham Omelet	Potato Cheese Croquettes	Asian Popcorn Chicken

CONCLUSION

With the growing demand for healthier cooking and better nutrition, people have turned to the air fryer as an alternative way of cooking without fat. After all, too much fat from fried foods in one's diet contributes to obesity and cardiovascular diseases. However, fat really does make food palatable. No wonder it's tough to give up that pleasant fried taste. With an air fryer, though, you capture the great taste of fried foods without the use of oil. It's a practical way for anyone striving to become slim and healthy.

Healthy food should not be a fad or an impossibility to choose; it should be part of everyone's life. Of course, this does not mean that you must give up enjoying the kitchen; neither of the many dishes that can be prepared healthy. To get it there are certain appliances that can help you and a lot: for example, an air fryer.

The concept of an air fryer is to fry food items in the air instead of oil. This revolutionary kitchen appliance uses superheated air that circulates to cook the food. This way, you don't have to dunk your food in sizzling hot fat just to achieve that crunch.

Regarding structure, an air fryer almost looks like a large rice cooker but with a front door handle. It has a removable chunky tray that holds the food to the air fried. It has an integrated timer to allow you to pre-set cooking times, and an adjustable temperature control so you can pre-set the best cooking temperature.

Different models offer different features, such as digital displays, auto-power shut-off, but mostly they work the same and use the same technology.

The air fryers have gained a lot of popularity over the last years due to their many advantages. Cooking in an air fryer is such a great and fun experience and you should try it as soon as possible.

The air fryer is such an innovative appliance that allows you to cook some of the best, most succulent and rich meals for you, your family and friends.

The air fryer reduces the cooking time and the effort you spend in the kitchen.

Having an air fryer is a great option. You can enjoy a healthier meal and save a good part of the oil expense, all without giving up enjoyable, fried foods.

Get a copy of this amazing air fryer cooking guide and use it to make real feast using this great appliance.

Start this culinary journey right away and enjoy the benefits of cooking with the air fryer.

CPSIA information can be obtained
at www.ICGtesting.com
Printed in the USA
BVHW051553130421
604814BV00004B/948